John Rutter CAROLS

O HOLY NIGHT

Thirteen sacred carols and
Christmas hymns for mixed voices

EDITED AND ARRANGED
BY JOHN RUTTER

MUSIC DEPARTMENT

OXFORD
UNIVERSITY PRESS

PREFACE

O HOLY NIGHT presents thirteen of the finest and best-loved sacred carols and Christmas hymns in choral arrangements which may be performed either separately or else as a sequence (with or without readings and prayers) forming a complete Christmas service or concert.

Each arrangement is complete in itself, so the suggested sequence (shown with readings and prayers on p. 58) can be shortened or altered to suit the needs of different choirs and occasions.

Five Christmas hymns are included, in arrangements for choir, congregation/audience, and organ or orchestra. The opening hymn, *O come, O come, Emmanuel,* is suitable for use as a processional introit. Five carols are arranged for unaccompanied choir, and four for choir with piano, organ, or orchestra.

Instrumentation for the accompanied items is listed at the foot of their first pages. The hymns are scored for full orchestra, but any of the woodwind, brass and percussion may be omitted if organ is available. The carols are scored for small orchestra. All the accompaniments may satisfactorily be played by piano or organ alone.

Companion volumes of the John Rutter Carols:

JOY TO THE WORLD! (fifteen sacred carols and Christmas hymns)
WE WISH YOU A MERRY CHRISTMAS (twelve secular carols and Christmas songs)

Note:
Orchestral scores and parts are available from Oxford University Press.

CONTENTS

Carols suitable for unaccompanied singing are marked thus: *

TITLE   PAGE

O come, O come, Emmanuel 1
French 15th-cent. arr. John Rutter

*Angels we have heard on high 4
French trad. arr. John Rutter

Angels, from the realms of glory 9
Henry Smart arr. John Rutter

*Ding dong! merrily on high 12
French 16th-cent. arr. Charles Wood

*What child is this? 13
English trad. arr. John Rutter

Good Christian men, rejoice 16
German 14th-cent. arr. John Rutter

The first Nowell 21
English trad. arr. John Rutter

Away in a manger 26
J.R. Murray arr. John Rutter

O holy night 30
(Cantique de Noël)
Adolphe Adam arr. John Rutter

*Joy to the world 43
Lowell Mason

*Three kings of Orient 44
J.H. Hopkins arr. John Rutter

Go, tell it on the mountain 46
American folk song arr. John Rutter

Hark! the herald angels sing 54
Mendelssohn arr. John Rutter

A service of readings and carols 58

O COME, O COME, EMMANUEL

for Mixed Voices, S.A.T.B., Congregation, with Organ*

Words 18th Century
Tr. J. M. NEALE

Melody from 15th-century
French Processional
arranged by JOHN RUTTER

* Instrumentation: 2Fl, 2Ob, 2Cl, Bsn, 2Hn, 2Tpt, 2Tbn, B. Tbn, Tba, Timp, Strings. Woodwind, brass and timp are optional if organ is available. Orchestral scores and parts are available

**If this hymn is used processionally, verse 1 may be sung unaccompanied by choir only.

VERSES 2 and 5

2. O come, thou Rod of Jes - se, free Thine own from Sa-tan's ty - ran-
5. O come, thou Key of Da - vid, come, And o-pen wide our hea - v'nly

-ny;   From depths of hell thy peo - ple save, And give them vic-t'ry o'er___ the
home; Make safe the way that leads_ on high, And close the path to mi - se-

VERSE 3

CHOIR UNACCOMPANIED

3. O come, thou Day-spring, come _ and cheer_ Our spi-rits by thine ad - vent here; Dis-perse the gloo-my clouds of night,_ And death's dark sha-dows put _ to flight. Re-joice! re-joice! Em - ma - nu-el Shall come to thee, O Is - ra - el.

ANGELS WE HAVE HEARD ON HIGH

for Mixed Voices, S. A. T. B., *a cappella*

French traditional carol
arranged by
JOHN RUTTER

Refrain for Verses 1 and 3

v. 3: rall.

- - - ri-a in ex - cel - sis De - o.
- - - ri - a in ex - cel - sis De - o.
- - - ri-a in ex - cel - sis De - o.
- - - ri - a in ex - cel - sis De - o.
— glo - - ri - a in ex-cel-sis De - o.

S.

A.
mp
Glo -

T.
mf
2. Shep-herds, why this ju - bi - lee? Why your joy-ous strains pro-long?

B.
mp
Glo - - ri - a, glo - - ri - a.

mf
Say what may the ti - dings be, Which in-spire your heav'n-ly song?

- - ri - a, glo - ri - a.

2nd Tenors
mf
Glo -

- ri-a   in ex - cel - sis De - o.

- ri - a   in __ ex - cel - sis __ De - o.

- ri-a   in ex - cel - sis De - o.

- ri - a   in _____ ex - cel - sis De - o.

- ri - a   in ex - cel - sis De - o.

S.
A.

f

3. Come to __ Beth - le - hem   and see   Him whose birth the __ an - gels sing;

T.
B.

. f

Back to p. 5 for Refrain

mp   *mf cresc.*   *f*

Come __ a - dore, __ on   bend - ed knee,   Christ, the Lord,   the __ new - born King.

Christ __

knee,   *mf cresc.*   *f*

ANGELS, FROM THE REALMS OF GLORY

for Mixed Voices, S. A. T. B., with Organ*

Words by
J. MONTGOMERY

HENRY SMART (1813-1879)
Verse 5 arranged by
JOHN RUTTER

Soprano
Alto

1. An - gels, from the realms of glo - ry, Wing your flight o'er
2. Shep-herds, in the field a - bid - ing, Watch-ing o'er your

Tenor
Bass

all the earth; Ye who sang cre - a - tion's sto - ry
flocks by night, God with man is___ now re - si - ding;

Now pro - claim Mes - si - ah's birth: *Come and wor - ship,*
Yon - der shines the___ in - fant light:

come and wor - ship, Wor - ship Christ___ the___ new - born King.

3. Sages, leave your contemplations;
Brighter visions beam afar;
Seek the great desire of nations;
Ye have seen his natal star:
Come and worship, come and worship,
Worship Christ the new-born King.

4. Saints before the altar bending,
Watching long in hope and fear,
Suddenly the Lord, descending,
In his temple shall appear:
Come and worship, come and worship,
Worship Christ the new-born King.

To next page for verse 5

*Instrumentation: 2Fl, 2Ob, 2Cl, Bsn, 2Hn, 2Tpt, 2Tbn, B. Tbn, Tba, Timp, Strings. Woodwind, brass and timp are optional if organ is available. Orchestral score and parts are available.

DING DONG! MERRILY ON HIGH

Words by
G.R. WOODWARD

16th c. French tune
harmonized by CHARLES WOOD

1. Ding dong! mer-ri-ly on high in heav'n the bells are ring-ing:
Ding dong! ve-ri-ly the sky is riv'n with an-gel sing-ing.

2. E'en so here be-low, be-low, let stee-ple bells be swung-en,
And *i - o, i - o, i - o,* by priest and peo-ple sung-en.

3. Pray you, du-ti-ful-ly prime your mat-in chime, ye ring-ers;
May you beau-ti-ful-ly rime your eve-time song, ye sing-ers.

Glo - - - - - - - - - - - - - - - - - ri-a, Ho-san-na in ex-cel-sis!

i-o pronounced *ee-o*

WHAT CHILD IS THIS?

for Mixed Voices, S. A. T. B., a cappella

Words by
W. C. DIX

English traditional melody
arranged by JOHN RUTTER

14

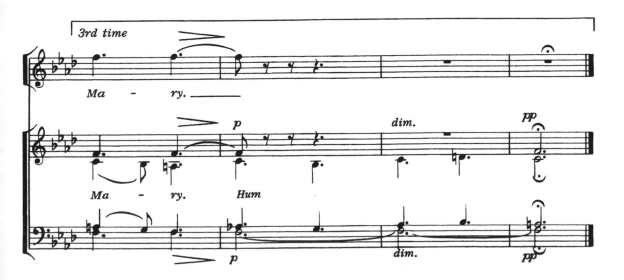

GOOD CHRISTIAN MEN, REJOICE

for Mixed Voices, S. A. T. B., with Keyboard*

Words by
J. M. NEALE

German, 14th century
arranged by
JOHN RUTTER

* Instrumentation: 2Fl/Picc, 2Ob, 2Cl, 2Bsn, 2Hn, Perc, Hp, Strings.
Orchestral scores and parts are available.
An unaccompanied arrangement of this melody to the text In dulci jubilo is included in the companion volume, Joy to the World!

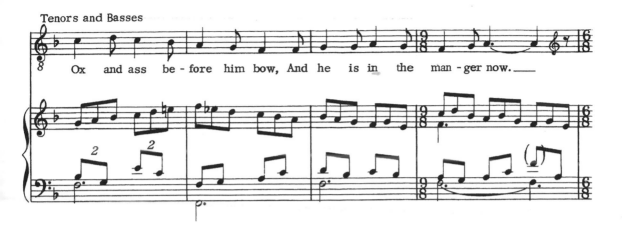

Ox and ass be - fore him bow, And he is in the man - ger now.___

Christ is born to - day!___ Christ is born to - day!___

2. Good Chris - tian men,___ re - joice___ With

heart and soul and voice; Now ye hear of end - less bliss:

Je - sus Christ was born for this! He has o - pened hea -ven's door, And

man is bless'd for ev - er-more. Christ was born for this!

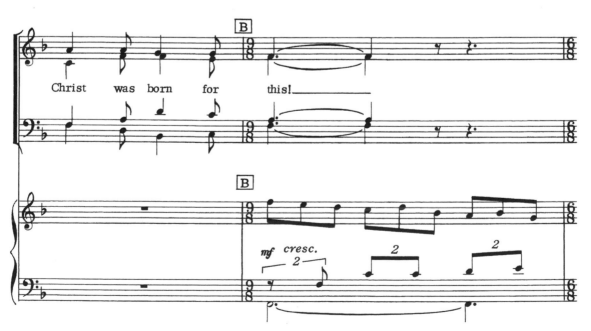

Christ was born for this!

All Voices

3. Good Chris - tian men, re - joice With heart and soul and voice;

Now ye need not fear the grave:___ Je - sus Christ was born to save!

THE FIRST NOWELL

for Mixed Voices, S. A. T. B., Congregation, with Organ*

English traditional carol
arranged by JOHN RUTTER

Verses 1, 3, and 5
Choir and Congregation

* Instrumentation: 2Fl, 2Ob, 2Cl, Bsn, 2Hn, 2Tpt, 2Tbn, B. Tbn, Tba, Timp, Perc, Strings. Woodwind, brass and percussion are optional if organ is available. Orchestral scores and parts are available.

earth_ it _ gave_great_ light, And_ so_ it con - tin-ued both_
did _ both_ stop_ and_ stay Right_ ov-er the place_ where_

Refrain
Choir and Congregation

day _ and night: *No - well, _ No - well, No - well, _ No -*
Je - sus lay: *No - well, _ No - well, No - well, _ No -*

V. 4: organ with voices

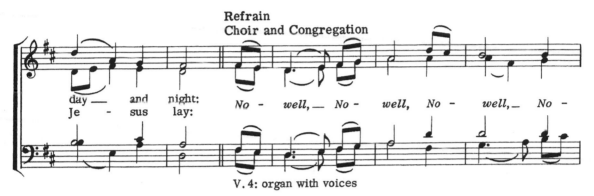

- well, _ Born_ is the King _ of Is - ra - el!

Verse 6

Choir 1 and Congrega-tion

Choir 2
(optional)

f
6. Then_ let _ us _ all with_ one_ ac - cord Sing_ prai - ses

f
6. Then let _ us _ all, then_ let _ us all _ with - one ac -

24

AWAY IN A MANGER

Words anon.*

Tune by
J. R. MURRAY
arranged by
JOHN RUTTER

-way in a man-ger, no crib for a bed, The lit - tle Lord

Je - sus laid down his sweet head. The stars in the bright sky looked

* First published in *A Little Children's Book for Schools and Families* (Lutheran, 1885)

Instrumentation: 2Fl, Hp, Strings. Orchestral scores and parts are available.
An unaccompanied setting of the same text to its original tune by W. J. Kirkpatrick is included in the companion volume Joy to the World!

down where he lay, The lit - tle Lord Je - sus a -sleep on the

hay.

unis. mp

2. The

A *p*

Aw _____ Aw _____

cat - tle are low -ing, the ba - by a - wakes, But lit - tle Lord

O HOLY NIGHT
(Cantique de Noël)
for Mixed Voices, S. A. T. B., with Organ*

Words by
CAPPEAU DE ROQUEMAURE

ADOLPHE ADAM (1803-1856)
arranged by JOHN RUTTER

*Instrumentation: 2Fl, Ob, 2Cl, Bsn, 2Hn, Hp, Strings. Orchestral scores and parts are available.
**Soprano part in verse 1 may be sung by a solo soprano or tenor.

night   of   the dear   Sa - vior's   birth;
Dieu   of   des - cen - dit   jus - qu'à   nous,

Long   lay the   world____   in sin   and er - ror
Pour   ef - fa - cer____   la tache   o - ri - gi-

pin -   ing,   Till he   ap - peared,   and the soul   felt   its
-nel -   le   Et de   son Père   ar - rê - ter   le   cour -

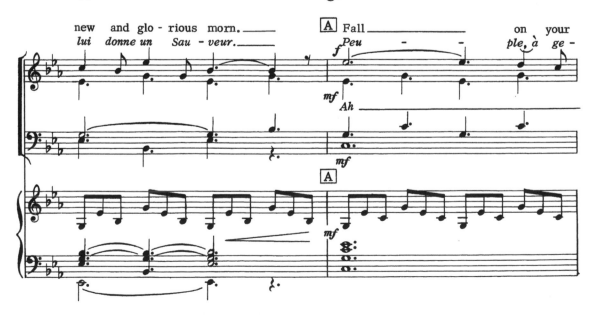

34

bro - ther, And in his Name___ all op-pres - sion shall
-cla - ve, *L'a-mour u - nit___ ceux qu'en-chaî - nait le*

cease.
fer.
Sweet hymns of joy in
Qui lui di - ra no -

grate - ful cho - rus raise we, Let all with - in us
-tre re-con - nais-san - ce? C'est pour nous tous qu'il

praise his ho - ly Name.____ Christ _____ is the
naît, qu'il souf-fre et meurt.____ Peu - - ple, de -

Lord, then ev - er, ev - er praise we, His
-bout, chan - te ta dé - li - vran - ce, No -

and glo - ry____ ev - er-more pro -
No - ël!____ chan - tons____ le Ré-demp-

pow'r _____ and glo - ry ev - er - more___ pro -
-ël! _____ No - ël! No - ël! No - ël!___ No -

and glo - ry ev - er - more pro -
No - ël! _____ No - ël, chan-tons No -

JOY TO THE WORLD!
(original version)

LOWELL MASON (1792–1872)
based on HANDEL

Words by ISAAC WATTS

3. No more let sins and sorrows grow,
Nor thorns infest the ground;
He comes to make his blessings flow
Far as the curse is found.

4. He rules the world with truth and grace;
And makes the nations prove
The glories of his righteousness
And wonders of his love.

An accompanied arrangement of this hymn, for choir, is included in the companion volume, Joy to the World!

THREE KINGS OF ORIENT
(unaccompanied version)
for Mixed Voices, S. A. T. B.

Words and Music by
J. H. HOPKINS
arranged by JOHN RUTTER

An accompanied arrangement of this carol is included in the companion volume, Joy to the World!

VERSES 2, 3, 4*

Caspar 2. Born a king on Beth - le - hem plain, Gold I
Melchior 3. Frank - in - cense to of - fer have I, In - cense
Balthazar 4. Myrrh is mine; its bit - ter per - fume Breathes a
(8va. lower)

bring to crown him a - gain, King ___ for ev - er,
owns a De - i - ty nigh, Prayer ___ and prais - ing,
life of ga - ther - ing gloom; Sor - row - ing, sigh - ing,

to REFRAIN

Ceas - ing nev - er, O - ver us all to reign:
All men rais - ing, Wor - ship him, God most high:
Bleed - ing, dy - ing, Sealed in the stone - cold tomb:

VERSE 5
f

5. Glo - rious now be - hold him a - rise, King, and
f

cresc.

God, and sa - cri - fice! ___ Heav'n sings Al - le -
cresc.

ff   dim.   to REFRAIN
                                    mf

-lu - ia: Al - le - lu - ia the earth ___ re - plies:
ff   dim.   mf

*If desired, choir may hum the parts of verse 5 during the singing of verses 2 and 3.
Verse 4 should be sung unaccompanied, an octave lower than verses 2 and 3.

GO, TELL IT ON THE MOUNTAIN

for Mixed Voices, S. A. T. B., with Piano*

American folk song
arranged by JOHN RUTTER

NOTE: This melody exists in several variant versions. As far as can
be ascertained, none of them is definitive, so the present
version has been chosen from personal preference.

*Instrumentation: 2Fl, 2Ob, 2Cl, 2Bsn, 2Hn, Timp, Perc, Pno (optional), Hp, Strings. Orchestral scores and parts are available.

shep-herds kept their watch-ing O'er si-lent flocks by night, Be-hold, through-out the hea-vens There shone a ho-ly light.

B Tempo I (♩ = 112)

Go, ___ tell it on the moun-tain, O-ver the hills and

(r. h. an 8ve higher ad lib.)

* If preferred, tenors may sing in unison with basses for the next eight measures.

Je - sus Christ_ is born. 3. Down in a low - ly

man - ger The hum - ble Christ was born, And

brought us God's sal - va - tion That bless - ed Christ - mas morn. _

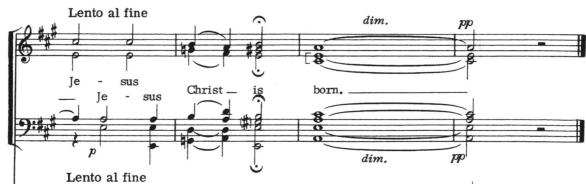

HARK! THE HERALD ANGELS SING

for Mixed Voices, S. A. T. B., with Organ*

Words by C. WESLEY
T. WHITEFIELD, M. MADAN
and others

MENDELSSOHN
Verse 3 arranged by
JOHN RUTTER

f 1. Hark! the he - rald an - gels sing__ Glo - ry to the new-born King;
mf 2. Christ, by high - est heav'n a - dored,__ Christ, the e - ver - last-ing Lord,

Peace on earth and mer - cy mild,__ God and sin - ners re - con-ciled:
Late in time be - hold him come__ Off-spring of a vir-gin's womb:

Joy - ful all ye na - tions rise,__ Join the tri - umph of the skies,__
Veiled in flesh the God-head see, — Hail th'in - car - nate De - i - ty! __

With th'an - gel - ic host pro-claim, Christ is __ born in Beth - le - hem.
Pleased as man with man to dwell, Je - sus __ our Em - ma - nu - el.

Hark! the he - rald an - gels sing Glo - ry __ to the new-born King.

Org.

Org. ped.

Melody and harmony for verses 1 and 2 adapted by W. H. Cummings (1831-1915) from a chorus by Mendelssohn.
*Instrumentation: 2Fl, 2Ob, 2Cl, 2Bsn, 2Hn, 2Tpt, 2Tbn, B. Tbn, Tba, Timp, Perc, Strings. Woodwind, brass and percussion are optional if organ is available. Orchestral scores and parts are available.

56

A SERVICE OF READINGS AND CAROLS

OPENING HYMN *O come, O come, Emmanuel*

BIDDING PRAYER *(spoken by the Minister)*

Beloved in Christ, be it at this Christmas-tide our care and delight to hear again the message of the angels, and in heart and mind to go even unto Bethlehem and see this thing which is come to pass, and the Babe lying in a manger.

Therefore let us read and mark in Holy Scripture the tale of the loving purposes of God and the glorious redemption brought us by this Holy Child.

But first, let us pray for the needs of the whole world; for peace on earth and goodwill among all his people; for unity and brotherhood within the Church he came to build, and especially in this our congregation.

And because this would rejoice his heart, let us remember, in his name, the poor and helpless, the cold, the hungry, and the oppressed; the sick and them that mourn, the lonely and the unloved, the aged and the little children; all those who know not the Lord Jesus, or who love him not, or who by sin have grieved his heart of love.

Lastly, let us remember before God all those who rejoice with us, but upon another shore, and in a greater light, that multitude which no man can number, whose hope was in the Word made flesh, and with whom in this Lord Jesus we for evermore are one.

These prayers and praises let us humbly offer up to the throne of heaven, in the words which Christ himself hath taught us:

THE LORD'S PRAYER *(spoken by all)*

CAROL *Angels we have heard on high*

HYMN *Angels, from the realms of glory*

READING St Matthew 1, vv. 18-23

CAROLS *Ding dong! merrily on high*
What child is this?
Good Christian men, rejoice

HYMN *The first Nowell*

READING St Luke 2, vv. 8-16

CAROLS *Away in a manger*
O holy night

HYMN *Joy to the world!*

READING St Matthew 2, vv. 1-11

CAROLS *Three kings of Orient*
Go, tell it on the mountain

READING St John 1, vv. 1-14

> *Minister* The Lord be with you
> *Congregation* And with thy spirit
> *Minister* Let us pray

THE COLLECT FOR CHRISTMAS EVE *(spoken by the Minister)*

O God, who makest us glad with the yearly remembrance of the birth of thy only Son, Jesus Christ: Grant that as we joyfully receive him for our Redeemer, so we may with sure confidence behold him, when he shall come to be our judge; who liveth and reigneth with thee and the Holy Spirit, one God, world without end. *Amen.*

THE BLESSING *(spoken by the Minister)*

May he who by his Incarnation gathered into one things earthly and heavenly, fill you with the sweetness of inward peace and goodwill; and the blessing of God Almighty, the Father, the Son, and the Holy Spirit, be upon you and remain with you always. *Amen.*

CLOSING HYMN *Hark! the herald angels sing*